Do you know where Oliver Cromwell lived, or where Wat Tyler was murdered, or John Wilkes born? What was 'the harvest of heads' on London Bridge? Where were Tyburn and Newgate? Who founded Bart's Hospital and why? Who else is buried in Highgate Cemetery? When did the Suffragettes smash the shop windows in Oxford Street?

Every year millions of people visit London and invariably head towards the traditional tourist attractions such as Westminster Abbey and the British Museum.

By contrast this guide focuses on 'the people's London', showing how Londoners have lived over the past 2000 years. It looks at famous churches, prisons, fairs, markets, meeting places and cemeteries, as well as individuals such as Wat Tyler, Oliver Cromwell, John Wilkes, Karl Marx and William Morris, and important episodes like the Peasants' Revolt and the Blitz.

The People's Guide to London provides a well-illustrated panorama of London life since the Romans, complete with maps, two useful indexes, the opening hours of places mentioned in the book, and a guide to further reading.

Andrew Davies *lectures for the Extra-Mural Departments at Cambridge and London Universities, the City University and the Workers' Educational Association, specialising in social history and the history of London. He has written a history of the 1940s,* Where Did The Forties Go? A Popular History *(Pluto Press, 1984), and in 1985 Macmillan will be publishing his survey of British theatre since 1800.*

A traffic jam at Ludgate Circus in the 1870s: *As drawn by Gustave Doré. 'For the real London-lover, the mere immensity of the place is a large part of its merit' — Henry James.*

The People's Guide to London

(Central and West End)

by
Andrew Davies

'The English are the worst people in the world, the most
obstinate and presumptuous, and of all England the Londoners
are the worst . . . for they are bold and courageous, and the
more their blood is spilled the greater is their courage.'

Jean Froissart, *a French cleric writing in the fourteenth century*

JOURNEYMAN

The Journeyman Press Limited
97 Ferme Park Road, Crouch End, London, N8 9SA,
and 17 Old Mill Road, West Nyack, NY 10994, USA

First published July 1984

1 2 3 4 5 6 7 8 9 printing

ISBN 0 904526 89 5

Cover design and text artwork by Peter Hammarling/Kathryn Tattersall
Picture research by Diana Korchien
Additional photographs by David Hoffman
Hand-drawn map by Louis Mackay

The cover illustration of Bartholomew Fair, 1721, has been reproduced by kind
permission of the Fotomas Index.

Text set in 10 on 11 Gill Light
Printed and bound in Great Britain

Acknowledgments

Scores of people have helped in the making of this book, both with their suggestions and encouragement, including: Pat Battell, Margaret and Chris Brunel, Jack Dywien, Max and Sadie Egelnick, Jo Florent, Ann Rossiter, Andrew Rothstein, Joe Shochat, Rachel Weinstein, and Nick Wetton. As always, I owe much to Jack Lindsay.

Many thanks to Fran Hazelton for her advice, the members of numerous adult education classes on London for putting me right when I went wrong, my parents and family for their unflagging support and faith in me, and Peter Sinclair for his enthusiasm and cheerfulness which made working with him on this book an instructive pleasure. Above all, thanks to Jean who has contributed in so many ways, not least in accompanying me on our walks around London visiting the places covered here, pointing out much that I would otherwise have missed.

Acknowledgments to illustrations

The publisher and author would like to thank the following for their kind permission to reproduce copyright illustrations:

BBC Hulton Picture Library: **54**bottom, **62**bottom, **66**left, **74**bottom, **77**both. British Museum: **10**. British Tourist Authority: **45**. Communist Party Picture Library: **58**left, **59**right, **61**top. Corporation of London: **4**top, **8**. Andrew Davies: **ii**, **20**, **23**top, **31**. Fotomas Index: **x**, **4**bottom, **6**, **9**, **18**top, **21**both, **24**top, **35**top, **38**, **43**, **48**, **51**top, **55**. GLC: **40**, **59**left, **69**bottom. Guildhall: **23**bottom, **30**. David Hoffman: **16**, **26**right, **71**, **73**. Peter Jackson: **7**, **14**, **18**bottom, **28**top, **35**bottom, **36**top, **46**, **61**bottom, **74**top. Magdalene College, Cambridge: **64**. Mansell Collection: **11**, **13**, **15**top, **19**, **22**, **24**bottom, **26**left, **27**, **29**, **32**, **33**, **34**both, **36**bottom, **37**, **39**, **42**, **44**both, **49**top, **51**bottom, **56**, **60**, **67**, **75**, **76**. Marx Memorial Library: **65**top, **70**left, **72**. Mary Evans Picture Library: **49**bottom. Museum of London: **3**. Network Photographers: **78**. Order of St. John: **12**. Popperfoto: **5**, **63**. Royal Opera House Archives: **52**, **54**top. Ianthe Ruthven: **65**bottom. St. Bartholomew's Hospital: **28**bottom left, **28**bottom right. Peter Sinclair: **58**right, **69**top, **70**right. Edwin Smith: **15**bottom. TUC Library: **62**top. William Morris Gallery: **66**right, **68**.

Our special thanks to the London Transport Executive for permission to use their map on page **86**, and to the British Tourist Authority for the use of their maps on pages **viii-ix**, **17**, **25**, **41**, **47**, **53** and **57**.

List of maps

Contents

Central and
West End of London

Nelson's Column: *Trafalgar Square was once the site of the royal stables. Finally put up in 1843 after many years delay, the Column was actually built by 'scab' labour because of the contractors' dispute with the stonemasons.*

Introduction

Tourism is one of the few industries which continues to flourish in modern Britain. In 1982-83 alone, for example, this country attracted nearly 13 million overseas visitors who spent between them over £3,000 million. About one million people are employed in jobs connected with the tourist industry.

Often it is 'the sights of London' which entice visitors, those traditional places normally used to convey a top-heavy view of London history, of kings and queens, statesmen, generals and members of the nobility. For instance, between two and three million people visit the British Museum, the Tower of London, St. Paul's Cathedral and Westminster Abbey each year.

London is also full of statues and memorials to our governors, and even the very names of its streets and squares derive from the wealthy and powerful: Leicester (Square) after the 2nd Earl of Leicester; Oxford (Street) after the Earl of Oxford; and Grosvenor (Square, Place, Road and Gate) after the Grosvenor family, also known as the Dukes of Westminster — these are just a few examples from literally hundreds.

By contrast, the great majority of Londoners who have lived, worked, struggled and entertained themselves over the past 2000 years been granted few testimonials.

This book represents a small step in trying to redress the imbalance, focusing on a London of fairs, pubs and meeting places, criminals and heretics, cemeteries and hospitals, prostitutes, immigrants and radicals, riots and marches. It deals with central and West End London, together with one or two spots in Hampstead and Highgate. Wherever possible I have tried to draw upon 'the voices of the past', letting people speak for themselves in their own words.

Clearly a book of this length can only be a beginning, but future volumes will fill in some of the gaps and concentrate on different areas of London. They are designed to be equally of use to those who wish to explore London in person or would rather sit and read about it. The illustrations and their captions are an integral part of each volume, and together with the text have been fully indexed.

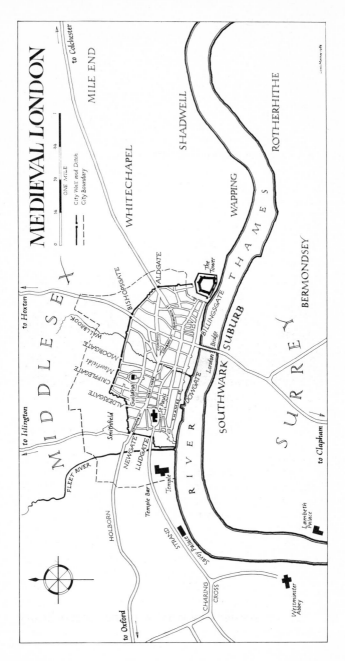

MEDIEVAL LONDON

ONE MILE

City Wall and Ditch
City Boundary

to Colchester

MILE END

to Hoxton

to Islington

to Oxford

MIDDLESEX

WHITECHAPEL

SHADWELL

WALLBROOK

BISHOPSGATE

ALDGATE

MOORGATE

CRIPPLEGATE

Moorfields

ALDERSGATE

Smithfield

Guildhall

St Paul's

NEWGATE

LUDGATE

Temple Bar

Temple

FLEET RIVER

HOLBORN

STRAND

SAVOY PALACE

CHARING CROSS

Westminster Abbey

to Clapham

The Tower

WAPPING

ROTHERHITHE

BILLINGSGATE

London Bridge

COWGATE

SOUTHWARK SUBURB

RIVER THAMES

SURREY

BERMONDSEY

Lambeth Palace

to Colchester

The early history

The origins of London are shrouded in mystery. There was certainly a settlement here on the banks of the river, probably with the use of a ferry or even a bridge, but our surviving evidence of early London remains scanty until the arrival of the Romans.

At first, Londinium was no more than a staging post used by traders, but it expanded rapidly — by AD 60 Tacitus was referring to it as '*a celebrated centre of commerce*'. However, it lacked any defences, and the next year Queen Boadicea and her followers razed the town to the ground. When rebuilding it the Romans recognised London's strategic importance by erecting a series of walls, the most permanent being constructed in the early fourth century around the town's 70,000 inhabitants, fragments of which can be seen today.

Roman wall at St. Alphage near the Barbican: *First built in the 2nd century AD, the Roman Wall encircled London until the late eighteenth century when it was largely destroyed.*

(Photographer: John Bailey)

In the early fifth century the Roman Empire began to disintegrate and the legions were brought home from far flung parts, leaving the fledgling city to look after itself. That departure signalled the arrival of the Dark Ages, in which information about almost anything is meagre.

But we do know that the people of London had rapidly established a reputation for bloody-minded independence. In 597, for example, Pope Gregory decided that because of the Londoners' intransigence Canterbury would be preferred as the ecclesiastical centre of England. In the ensuing centuries London was frequently besieged, and on the rare occasions when it was defeated — as in 851 when the Danes destroyed it — the city was soon rebuilt, in this case by Alfred the Great.

The Norman invasion

But in 1066 the invaders came for good. Defeating Harold at Hastings, William the Conqueror marched quickly to the north of London, and, by cutting off the city's food supplies, forced it to surrender. Although William had won this battle, he was all too aware of the resilience of London's inhabitants and it was by no means a one-sided peace.

On the one hand, William granted a charter to the capital which awarded certain privileges, virtually making it a city-state; its citizens had the right to elect their own sheriff, to maintain their own law courts, and to enjoy the income from the county of Middlesex.

William I's Charter: *'I give you to know, that ye be of all those Laws worthy that ye were in King Edward's day. And I will suffer no man to do you any wrong. God keep you.'*

On the other hand, the Norman barons were building castles all over the country to protect themselves, and in

London William built the Tower of London, placed just outside the east end of the city wall and designed to intimidate its people. The White Tower, which still exists, was finished by Gundulf, the Bishop of Rochester, in 1097.

The City of London was often in a strong position because of its financial strength, forcing a usually impecunious king to come to them cap in hand. Some of the concessions it extracted from the monarchy included the right of sole legal authority and the right to arrest and punish offenders

The White Tower: *The Tower of London rapidly acquired a variety of roles, as royal menagerie (until the animals were presented to the new Regent's Park Zoo in 1831), ammunition dump, treasure trove, record office and prison.*

within the gates. The aldermen were also allowed to choose the Mayor. The City's independence was commemorated until recently by a symbolic ritual: the sovereign on reaching the city boundary at Temple Bar could proceed no further until the Lord Mayor handed over the Sword of State which was then returned.

The Lord Mayor with the City Sword leaving St. Paul's: *Such ritual might appear antiquated and meaningless, but in fact it is symbolic of the city's proud self-consciousness.*

William Fitzstephen's history of London, written in 1174, portrayed a tranquil city: '*The only plagues of London are the immoderate drinking of fools, and the frequency of fires.*' He failed to mention that the people were used to taking part in turbulent political debates, usually in the vicinity of St. Paul's. A folkmote or meeting was held from Norman times in the open space to the east of the churchyard, with the citizens discussing and then voting upon current issues. At the north-east corner stood St. Paul's Cross — marked today by a column with St. Paul on the top — which consisted of a timber pulpit facing a congregation that was either standing or seated on stools. Sermons were preached here from the 1250s, and inevitably religious matters became closely linked to political controversy, especially when John Wyclif and the Lollards attacked the corruption of the church.

Londoners might have been united against any encroachments on their liberties planned by the King at Westminster, but there were divisions within the city itself. In particular, the 'burghers' of the merchant guilds were adamant that the craftsmen should remain unrepresented inside the guilds, denying them any right in deciding how the trade was to be conducted. One outburst of this simmering conflict between rich and poor came towards the end of the twelfth century.

William Longbeard's revolt

In 1196 William Longbeard, a magistrate and an eloquent orator, held a series of meetings at which he denounced the greed of the wealthy in pilfering from the revenues. He also objected to the special tax levied to pay for the ransom needed to free Richard I from captivity on the continent, and singled out for especial criticism the aldermen, many of whose appointments were now hereditary and unelected.

An eyewitness account noted the kind of things William was saying, often from St. Paul's Cross: *'Do you, oh poor! who have experienced the heaviness of the rich man's hand, drink from my wells the waters of the doctrine of salvation, and ye may do this joyfully, for the time of your visitation is at hand. For I will divide the waters from the waters. The people are the waters. I will divide the humble from the haughty and treacherous. I will separate the elect from the reprobate, as the light from darkness.'*

St. Paul's Cross: *Folkmotes or debates were held here from the twelfth century. The Cross was pulled down by the Puritans in 1643. The present column with St. Paul on the top was erected in 1910.*

Finally the authorities decided that Longbeard was too dangerous to remain at large, and Archbishop Hubert sent a contingent of soldiers to arrest him. Two of the troops were killed in the ensuing scuffle, and Longbeard, together with some followers and his mistress, '*who clave to him with inseparable constancy*', fled to St. Mary-le-Bow in Cheapside.

This church had been built in the 1080s and was the first in the city to have been constructed on arches of stone. Like all other churches it offered a place of sanctuary. However Archbishop Hubert ignored this long-standing custom and instructed the church to be set on fire, forcing Longbeard out

St. Mary-le-Bow, Cheapside: *Anyone born within the sound of this church's 'Bow Bells' is a 'cockney'. The word was originally a term of contempt, a cockney being a hen's egg.*

— whereupon he was quickly stabbed to death. His body was hung on a gibbet at Tyburn along with nine of his followers as a warning to the populace not to get ideas above their station.

But this was not the end of the matter. The poor looked upon Longbeard as having been their saviour and began to scrape away the earth under the gallows in the belief that it would help to heal diseases. Soldiers had to be called to disperse the crowds.

One historian of the time, Matthew Paris, who was a monk at St. Alban's, summed up the whole episode: '*Thus William of the Beard was shamefully put to death by his fellow citizens for asserting the truth and defending the cause of the poor; and if the justice of one's cause constitutes a martyr, we may surely set him down as one.*'

Magna Carta and Simon de Montfort

Within twenty years of Longbeard's death London found itself once more in turmoil. This time it was the barons fighting against the arbitrary powers of King John, who eventually had to concede the Magna Carta of 1215. This document confirmed the city's independence: '*The City of London shall have all its ancient liberties and free customs, as well by land and by water.*'

But later kings, particularly Henry III, lacked any intention of observing its provisions, and in his desire to finance a wealthy court and foreign adventures Henry was not too concerned how he raised money. Demands grew that he should at least listen to the views of the people, and in the Provisions of Oxford of July 1258 it was agreed that the Great

The Magna Carta: *Signed by King John and the barons at Runnymede beside the Thames in 1215, it established certain liberties, in particular that 'No freeman shall be taken or imprisoned . . . except by the lawful judgments of his peers or the law of the land.'*

London Bridge in 1500: *A popular and often fatal occupation was the 'shooting of the rapids' under the Bridge. Jousting tournaments were also held along its length.*

Council should assemble three times a year. When it did, '*the Commonalty shall elect twelve honest men who shall come to the Parliaments, and at other times when occasion shall be when the King and his Council shall send for them, to treat of the wants of the King and of his Kingdom.*' Already the beginnings of the House of Commons can be detected.

But once again Henry blatantly ignored the Provisions, prompting Simon de Montfort and several other barons to rise against him. In 1264 de Montfort and his army were stranded in Southwark, barred from London by the prosperous burghers. Hearing of a surprise attack on de Mortfort by the king, and summoned by the bells of St. Paul's, the poorer people lowered the drawbridge on London Bridge and allowed de Montfort's men access to the city.

The next year de Montfort was killed in battle, but he had succeeded in calling a Parliament and thus shifting the arguments about popular representation onto a new and more secure level. And, as a contemporary 'Chronicle' vividly demonstrates, his example lived on: '*As the news of his death ran through the land there was a stopping of laughter, and a universal lamentation arose until later the sighs changed to hymns of praise and joy because of the numerous miracles said to have been caused by his unconquerable inflexibility and patience and purity of faith, and thereby was hope aroused of escaping from the oppression of the wicked.*'

But all of these episodes pale into insignificance beside the Peasants' Revolt of 1381.

The Peasants' Revolt

Feudalism in England

In the Middle Ages England was under the sway of the feudal system, a division of society which separated the numerous serfs from the few lords. The serfs owed many onerous dues to their lord: they had to work his land several days of the year without payment; their children could not marry without his permission; and serfs were unable to move from the village where they were brought up.

However the Black Death of the late 1340s transformed the situation. The death of a third of the population resulted in a subsequent shortage of labourers. Serfs began to insist that they were paid in money for their work and demanded ever-higher wages. Parliament tried to prevent this by passing the Statute of Labourers in 1351 — probably the first incomes policy in history — but was unsuccessful.

At the same time the English kings were fighting the Hundred Years War in France and its huge costs meant that taxes had to be increased, as they were in 1379 and 1380. Opposition to these new measures spread throughout the country, encouraged by the large number of rebel priests who were touring the rural districts and arguing that Christianity was about equality, toleration and fellowship here on earth. In the words of one of them, John Ball: *'When Adam delv'd and Eve span/Who was then the gentleman?'*

Adam and Eve: *The popular saying above was used by travelling preachers such as John Ball: if there were no lords and masters at the beginning of time, why do they exist now?*

The march on London

By 1381 southern England was in ferment, and the attempt by government inspectors to gather in the taxes sparked off a series of riots and risings, especially in Essex and Kent. In the summer of that year the peasants decided to march upon London and present their grievances to the King, Richard II.

Although the following series of events are usually called the Peasants' Revolt, the protest included much broader groupings of people than exclusively peasants. Above all, however, the movement was well-disciplined and their leaders, such as Wat Tyler, Jack Straw, John Ball and Will Grindcrobbe, were highly articulate and persuasive spokesmen.

The two contingents from Essex and Kent began to converge on London in June. The men from the south paused in Southwark to burn down the multitude of brothels, freeing the women, many of whom had been brought over from France. The men from the north stopped in Highbury to ransack the residence of the Prior of St. John, Sir Robert Hales. They had good reason for singling out Hales. He was the official responsible for the harsh enforcement of the poll tax which had led to the rising — earning him the popular nickname 'Hob the Robber' — and in addition lived in ostentatious splendour, a contemporary calling his Highbury mansion *'as good as the Garden of Eden'*. The Essex section then marched to Clerkenwell where they destroyed the Priory of St. John itself, camping out on Clerkenwell Green.

Priory Church of St. John: *The early London historian Fitzstephen reckoned that there were 126 churches in the capital by the late twelfth century; this was founded in the 1140s.*

St. John's Gate in 1870: *Restored in 1504 the Gate later housed the office of the Master of Revels which handled the question of theatre censorship, and it is probable that Shakespeare was a visitor. It later contained the 'Gentleman's Magazine', and then a tavern and coffee house, Hogarth's father being one of the proprietors.*

London was still protected at this time by the wall, but many of its inhabitants sympathised with the revolt and allowed the East Anglian men to enter through Aldgate (coincidentally the poet Chaucer was living just above the gate). In the south four aldermen lowered the drawbridge on London Bridge.

Once again their vengeance was highly selective. The lawyers' lodgings at the Temple were destroyed, along with the feudal records, and the Savoy Palace, home of the hated John of Gaunt, was burnt down. There was no looting; one man found trying to steal from the burning palace was thrown back into the flames.

Two meetings with the King

The next day, June 14th, the men, led by Wat Tyler, gathered on the open fields of Mile End to parley with the young Richard II and his advisers. Their demands were succinct and reasonable: cuts in taxation and the replacement of Richard's *'evil councillors'*. Richard and his party faced two problems: first the huge mass of people confronting them — estimates of which varied between 60,000 and 100,000 — and secondly the fact that the royal army was campaigning miles away in the north. Their ploy was to play for time, so Richard agreed to the rebels' requests.

He commanded his thirty clerks to begin preparing the charters, setting their tables up in Cheapside, outside St. Mary-le-Bow. Charles Poulsen, in his book **The English Rebels**, quotes from one of these charters for the area around Hertford:

Aldgate: *Originally called 'Old Gate', it was rebuilt on several occasions and finally removed in the 1760s when, like the other gates, it was obstructing the increased flow of traffic.*

'Know that by our special grace we have manumitted all our liegemen, subjects and others of the county of Hertford; and we have freed and quitted each of them from bondage by the present letters. We also pardon our said liege men and subjects for all felonies, acts of treason, transgressions and extortions performed by them or any one of them in whatsoever way. We also withdraw sentences of outlawry declared against them or any of them because of these offences. And we hereby grant our complete peace to them and each of them.'

Theoretically, such charters meant the end of feudalism.

The rebels continued to attack well-deserved targets, like the Fleet and Newgate prisons, both of which were renowned for their barbaric conditions; an official inquiry into the treatment of the prisoners in Newgate in 1334 revealed how *'All were alike threatened, many tortured, till they yielded to the keeper's extortions, or consented to turn approvers and* swear away the lives of innocent men. These poor prisoners were dependent upon the charity and good will of the benevolent for food and raiment.'

They also gained access to the Tower of London, which they could only have managed with the support of its guards,

Sudbury and Hales being dragged out to Tower Hill, 1381: *A contemporary chronicler described the bungling of the Archbishop's murder; his executioners hacked away at him until 'being mangled with eight several strokes in the neck and head, he fulfilled most worthy martyrdom.'*

and there captured Sir Robert Hales, Archbishop Sudbury and two other men. They were promptly dragged out to Tower Hill and beheaded. Although this may seem unnecessarily bloodthirsty it is worth remembering, as A.L. Rowse has written, that it was 'a small number for such an upheaval: the mob was more merciful than the governing class, when it recovered its nerve.'

After the grant of the charters many of the rebels did indeed, as the king and his supporters hoped, leave London, and when a second meeting was held on June 15th the number of Tyler's men had been severely depleted. They confronted each other at St. John's Fields, close to where the priory had

The death of Wat Tyler: *Thomas Paine once wrote: 'If the Barons merited a monument in Runnymede, Wat Tyler merits one at Smithfield.'*

The Lord Mayor's dagger: *Supposedly the dagger with which William Walworth stabbed Tyler to death. It is kept in the Fishmongers' Hall.*

stood until a few days before. But this time it was the king's men who held the upper hand, and they succeeded in luring Tyler away from his followers. There were angry words, a fight started and, as planned, the Lord Mayor, William Walworth, stabbed Tyler, who was carried off mortally wounded to nearby Bart's Hospital. Walworth followed, pulling Tyler out of the hospital and into what is now West Smithfield and there cut off his head.

By then it was all over. The rebels, unable to see what had befallen Tyler, found themselves surrounded by the king's soldiers and dispersed in confusion back to their homes. But if they thought themselves secure and in 'complete Peace' after their charters, they were wrong. Richard and his men embarked upon a harsh programme of reprisals, and the contempt with which his circle looked upon the rest of the population is conveyed by the tone of his reply on being reminded of his former promises: 'Oh, you wretched men, detestable by land and sea, you who seek equality with lords and not worthy to live ... You will remain in bondage, not as before, but incomparably harsher. For as long as we live and by God's grace, rule over this realm, we will strive with mind, strength and wealth to suppress you so that the rigour of your servitude will be an example of posterity.' Scores of people were put to death.

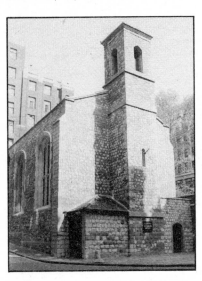

The Savoy Chapel:
Savoy Palace in the Strand was built in 1245. Restored after the Peasants' Revolt it was later a hospital, a refuge for debtors and a school. Parts of the Savoy Chapel date from 1505. The site was largely cleared when Waterloo Bridge was being constructed in the early nineteenth century, but the name lingers on in that of the Savoy Hotel.

A gallant failure

It might seem that the revolt of 1381 ended in depressing failure, the hopes and promises of June destroyed on the gallows, but that would be short-sighted. The authorities had been given a severe fright by the strength and organisation of the rebellion and never again would they be able to govern in complete defiance of the people. As G.M. Trevelyan concluded in his **English Social History**: '*the spirit that had prompted the rising was one of the chief reasons why serfdom died out in England, as it did not die out on the Continent of Europe.*'

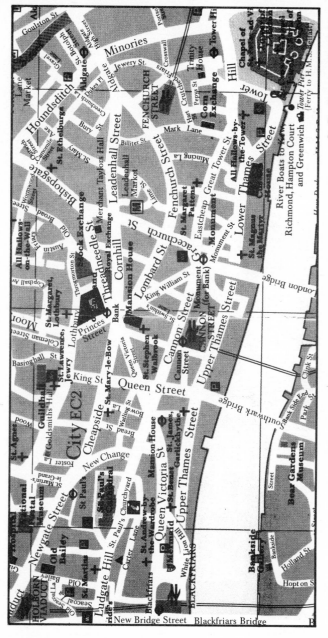

St. Paul's to London Bridge

Cheapside in 1702: *The Bow Bells of St. Mary-le-Bow inspired Dick Whittington to turn back again to London in 1375. The church was rebuilt by Wren after it had burnt down in the Great Fire; however the crypt, dating from 1070, remains to this day.*

Cheapside

For several centuries the most important London market was held in Cheapside, just to the east of St. Paul's. The name itself derives from the old English word 'ceap' or market, and the range of merchandise on sale there can still be gauged from the names of nearby streets: Bread Street (where John Milton was born in 1608), Honey Lane, Ironmonger Lane, and Milk Street (Sir Thomas More was born here in 1478).

Cheapside was the focus of London life during the Middle Ages, a meeting-place which also hosted activities ranging from business transactions to executions. Jousts and tournaments were also held here, and later on it was infamous for riots caused by the rowdy behaviour of apprentices and students.

The whole area suffered badly in

Cheapside Cross: *Edward I erected a series of crosses in honour of his dead wife Eleanor at each place where her body rested on its way to Westminster. The last halt was at Charing Cross.*

Cheapside in the 1880s: *At this time Cheapside still maintained a reputation for its fashionable shops. Note the omnibus in the photograph, a service introduced in 1829 between Paddington Green and the Bank. The first motorbus service was started in 1899.*

the Great Fire of 1666 and Samuel Pepys recorded sadly in his **Diary** for 5 September 1666, '*Thence homeward, having passed through Cheapside and Newgate Market, all burned*'. But Cheapside was rebuilt and in the next two centuries established a reputation for its goldsmiths and drapers, although the development of the West End shopping district by the close of the nineteenth century diminished Cheapside's significance.

Bartholomew Fair and Smithfield

Two or three hundred years ago every town and village used to hold an annual fair. Without the benefits of television, cinema, department stores or organised sport, the fair was the highlight of the year for local people, eagerly awaited and immensely enjoyed. Normally it provided a mix of both trading and pleasure activities, a proliferation of tents, sideshows and stalls offering cattle, sheep and cheese for sale, jostled together with strolling players, freaks and magicians. Although temporary and ephemeral, fairs sometimes had lasting consequences: for example, the origin of the name 'May/fair'.

The first major fair was Bartholomew Fair held in Smithfield from the 1130s. Smithfield was then just outside the city wall and mainly an area of farms and fields — originally called 'Smooth Field'. Ideal for markets and trading, William Fitzstephen described it in 1174 as: 'A smooth field where every Friday there is a celebrated rendezvous of fine horses to be sold, and in every quarter are placed vendibles of the peasant, swine with their deep flanks, and cows and oxen of immense bulk.'

For centuries cattle was sold here, the beasts wandering all over the surrounding streets with the kind of unfortunate consequences Charles Dickens outlined in **Oliver Twist**: 'The ground was covered, nearly ankle-deep with filth and mire, a thick steam perpetually rising from the reeking bodies of the cattle, and mingling with the fog.' After generations of complaint, the new (and present) Smithfield Market was completed in 1868, and a Poultry Market later added in 1963.

Smithfield had a bad reputation throughout the Middle Ages, one contemporary describing it as 'very foul, and like a marsh, and at all times it abounded in filth and muddy water; the part which was above water was allotted to the hanging of thieves.' Executions and burnings continued to be held here until the seventeenth century; memorials to some of the martyrs killed in Smithfield can be seen on the outer wall of Bart's Hospital.

Smithfield Market: *Its heyday was in the 1850s before the effects of the railway were felt, when over one and a half million sheep were sold each year.*

As for Bartholomew Fair itself, legend has it that a man called Rahere. formerly a court jester, decided to undertake a pilgrimage to Rome. Whilst on his journey he contracted malaria and seemed certain to die — until, that is, he saw a vision of St. Bartholomew who promised Rahere that he would recover if on his return to England he founded a church and a hospital. This he did: the church is St. Bartholomew the Great, and the hospital, Bart's.

The burning of martyrs at Smithfield: *During the reign of Mary Tudor some 270 Protestants were burned at the stake for their beliefs.*

Rahere needed to find some way of financing both church and hospital, so he prevailed upon his former employer, Henry II, to grant a charter for a fair with the tolls or tax going to the church. The Fair was first held in 1133 and soon attracted traders and merchants from all over Europe, the most important business indicated by one of today's neighbouring streets: Cloth Fair. Held every August for around two weeks, the Fair was a huge jamboree with

Cloth Fair: *The name of this street underlines the importance of the cloth and wool trade at Bartholomew Fair. Nearby is Bartholomew Close where John Milton sheltered in 1661 after the Restoration in fear of his life.*

its own customs and procedures — there was even a 'Court of Pie Powder' to settle disputes on the spot.

The Fair was an opportunity for people to let off steam, and the showmen did not miss a chance to comment on topical matters. In 1697 a William Philips was publicly whipped for his jests at the Fair satirising the government, and from 1700 there was friction with the Lord Mayor over a series of plays poking fun at the authorities.

Many writers have left their impressions of this impermanent event. Ben Jonson wrote a play entitled *Bartholomew Fair.* Samuel Pepys was there (he saw '*monkeys dancing on the ropes*', '*such dirty sport that I was not pleased with it*'); as, too,

22

A London street brawl: *Until the early nineteenth century there was no system of policing apart from the Bow Street Runners — originated by the brothers Fielding — and the generally incompetent 'Watch'.*

was William Wordsworth with his friend Charles Lamb in 1802. He also was not impressed as **The Prelude** demonstrates, describing it as:

> *This Parliament of Monsters.*
> *Tents and Booths*
> *Meanwhile, as if the whole were one vast mill,*
> *Are vomitting, receiving, on all sides,*
> *Men, Women, three-years' Children, Babes in Arms.'*

By this time, however, many of the fairs were in prolonged dispute with the forces of law and order and some — such as Southwark and Mayfair — had already ended in the 1760s. In particular, officialdom was worried by the political implications of huge numbers congregating together.

Bartholomew Fair poster:
This gives an indication of the amazing variety of entertainments which took place at this fair.

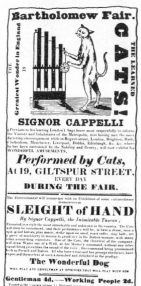

Greenwich Fair was still attracting 200,000 people in 1838.

Bartholomew Fair and its showmen faced continual harassment and rising rents, and it came to a sad end in 1855. Up and down the country it was a similar story and the Fairs Act of 1871 brought many of them to a close — although some like St. Giles in Oxford and the Goose Fair in Nottingham continue to be held. Ironically enough the rowdy and bucolic fair was replaced by the tea-drinking and genteel fête, yet again an attempt to raise money for a local church.

Cloth Fair and Middle Street: *This building was supposed to be as old as the priory of St. Bartholomew. At various times it had been a butchers, a haircutters and a pub.*

Bartholomew Fair in 1808: *This illustration by Pugin and Rowlandson emphasises the fact that Bartholomew Fair was as busy at night as during the day. The booth in the middle belongs to John Richardson, the most famous of the nineteenth-century strollers.*

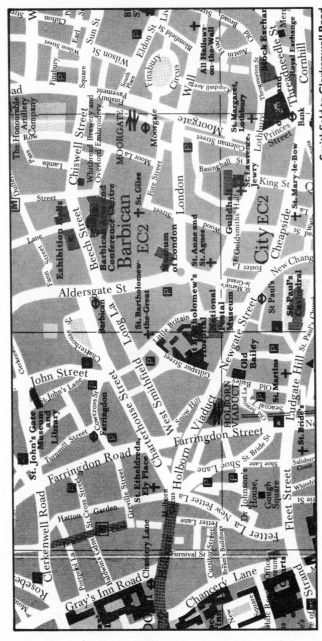

25

St. Bartholomew the Great

St. Bartholomew the Great, founded in 1123 by Rahere, is now the oldest parish church in London. The usual method of financing churches in the Middle Ages was by gifts from pilgrims, and few ecclesiastics could resist the temptation of increasing their establishment's popularity by forging a clutch of sacred relics. At St. Paul's a cache of holy objects was discovered in 1314. These were sold off over the years and surprisingly proved to be inexhaustible — as late as the 1450s the cathedral still boasted of possessing a portion of the Blessed Virgin's milk and the hand of St. John. Rahere did likewise, only later to be denounced as an imposter: his tomb can still be seen inside the church.

The church was once much larger than it is today, the nave originally stretching to the road; now the visitor has to make do with the attractive gatehouse in Little Britain built in 1559. After the Reformation of the 1530s parts of the church were used as a blacksmith, printer (where Benjamin Franklin worked), stable, school and public house.

Yet its trials were still not over by the time of the twentieth century: nearby Bartholomew Close — where the painter William Hogarth was born in 1697 and then baptised in the church — was bombed in a Zeppelin raid in 1916, during the Blitz in 1941 and again in 1944.

St. Bartholomew the Great. *It survived the Great Fire of 1666 and is thus the oldest parish church in the city by some 500 years.*

The gateway in Little Britain: *During a Zeppelin raid of 1916 the tiles above the gateway slid away to reveal this half-timbered Elizabethan house dating from 1595.*

Bart's Hospital and St. Bartholomew the Less

St. Bartholomew's Hospital was opened in the 1120s with Alfune, who later built St. Giles Cripplegate, as its first proctor. It is therefore London's oldest hospital. The monks and sisters who first cared for the poor also looked after the inhabitants of Newgate Prison.

In 1546 Bart's was refounded by Henry VIII and along with three others — Bethlem, Bridewell and St. Thomas's — it was known as a Royal Hospital. The 'refoundation' set up a Board of Governors, later to include William Hogarth whose murals of the Good Samaritan and the Pool of Bethesda now adorn the inside of the building.

Until the eighteenth century medical provision in London was rudimentary, but in that century five new hospitals were created: the Westminster Hospital was founded in 1720, Guy's in 1721, St. George's in 1733, the London in 1740, and the Middlesex in 1745. The dispensary movement also got under way, the first being started in Red Lion Square in 1769 for 'the Infant Poor'.

The major development in recent years has been the introduction of the National Health Service in 1948, a system based on the principle of medical aid for need and not payment.

St. Bartholomew the Less is the parish church of the hospital and stands in the corner of its grounds. Another building that suffered during the Blitz, it still retains its fifteenth-century tower.

Bart's Hospital: *The only one of the medieval hospitals still to be standing on its original site, the chief physician from 1609-1633 was William Harvey who discovered the circulation of the blood.*

Burnings outside Bart's Hospital: *The Scottish patriot William Wallace was one of those executed here, in 1305. A memorial to him stands on the outer wall of the hospital.*

St. Bartholomew the Less: *The great architect and designer Inigo Jones was baptised in this church in 1573. It escaped the Great Fire.*

Gatehouse of Bart's Hospital: *This gatehouse with its statue of Henry VIII was built in 1702, and the buildings in the quadrangle behind a few years later.*

Jack Cade's Revolt of 1450

The Peasants' Revolt was not the only rising during the Middle Ages. London had remained a turbulent and violent city with frequent riots, mainly because of the miserable living conditions. A vivid portrayal of London destitution is given by the sixteenth-century observer, Philip Stubbes: '*The poor lie in the streets upon pallets of straw, and well if they have that too, or else in the mire and dirt as commonly it is seen, having neither house to put in their heads, covering to keep them from cold, nor yet to hide their shame withal, penny to buy them sustenance, nor anything else, but are suffered to die in the streets like dogs or beasts, without any mercy or shame showed to them at all.*'

In the 1440s the country was enduring once more the privations of 'bad counsellors' and high taxation; bribery and extortion by officials was almost a way of life. But in 1450 a rising occurred in Kent led by Jack Cade, also known as 'Jack Amend-All' or 'The Captain of Kent'.

Cade had been a soldier of some ability and used his experience to instil a sense of discipline and unity amongst his followers. Numbering around 20,000, they were far from constituting a rabble — including squires, clergy and craftsmen in their ranks — and democratically elected their own captains, some of whom took names such as 'Robin Hood'. The list of grievances drawn up by them, 'The Complaint of the Poor Commons of Kent', attacked the widespread misgovernment, the Statute of Labourers for trying to restrain wages, and the iniquities of the legal system.

The petition was rejected out of hand by the government and an army sent to quell this disturbance, which, to the surprise of everyone except Cade's men, was defeated at Sevenoaks. By now

Jack Cade and London Stone, 1450: *When Jack Cade passed London Stone in Cannon Street, thought to date back to the Romans, he is supposed according to Shakespeare to have hit it with his sword and exclaimed of himself: 'Now is Mortymer lord of this city'.*

the men of Kent had been joined by others from neighbouring counties. The spread of social and political protest throughout the country was illustrated by a passage in the **Sherborne Annals** of Dorset: *'Though Jack made his march on London, the community of the realm was filled with infamy and those who feared neither King nor Law set up for themselves Captains in divers places to spoil ecclesiastics and the rich.'*

Reaching Southwark with his followers on July 1st and installing his headquarters at the White Hart, Cade insisted that order should be maintained, as the chronicler Hall recounted, *'prohibiting to all men murder, rape or robbery; by which colour he allured to him all the hartes of the common people.'*

Within the city of London, reaction to Cade's march was mixed. Those sympathetic to king and nobility had left; the broad majority welcomed him and lowered the drawbridge. When Cade's men entered the capital, their vengeance, as in 1381, was discriminate. Lords Saye and Crowmer were

The Guildhall: *The centre of the government of the City of London for hundreds of years, parts of the Guildhall date back to the 1410s but the building suffered severely during both the Great Fire and the Blitz.*

London Bridge in 1600: *For centuries London Bridge was the only passage over the Thames, until Westminster Bridge was opened in 1750. It was also an important shopping centre.*

captured at the Tower of London: Saye was tried at the Guildhall before being beheaded by Cade at the Standard conduit outside St. Mary-le-Bow in Cheapside; Crowmer was executed at Mile End. Other trials of corrupt officials were held at the Guildhall, and the Fleet, Marshalsea and King's Bench prisons thrown open.

There was no disorder or looting during the three days that the rebels held London — coincidentally the same length of time as in 1381. But the City Council, an organisation dominated by the more prosperous and conservative citizens, had already begun to manoeuvre for the removal of this 'occupying' army, and on the evening of July 5th they tried to raise the drawbridge on London Bridge, still the only thoroughfare over the Thames. Cade and his men fought to keep it lowered and the battle lasted well into the early morning. Finally, after twelve hours' fighting and with the drawbridge on fire, a truce was agreed.

By July 7th when Cade and some of his supporters met the Archbishop of Canterbury and several other clergy at St. Margaret's Church, Southwark, the rebel army was fading away, now that they heard news of the rapid advance of a royal army. The archbishop pledged that the rebels' demands would be discussed and to procure a general pardon for all those involved. Some pardons were in fact granted, but not for Cade. He was declared an outlaw as he retreated south, and on July 12th was trapped and killed near Lewes in Sussex. His corpse was brought back to London and dismembered.

The government's reaction was merciless. Several acts were passed which heaped abuse on the dead Cade — 'horrible, wikked and heynous traytour and tiraunt' — and Henry VI hunted down anyone suspected of involvement in the rising. Those caught were executed and their heads placed on London Bridge, a series of reprisals which became known as 'the harvest of heads'.

Cade's revolt was followed during the next two hundred years by further Tudor rebellions, often weakened by popular reluctance to take up arms against the monarch. But that was to change in the seventeenth century.

The heads on London Bridge: *Sir Thomas More's head ended up here in 1535. His daughter Margaret bribed the bridge-keeper to drop it into a passing boat, and it was then decently buried.*

The Seventeenth and Eighteenth Centuries

The number of churches mentioned in the first sections of this book reflects the crucial role that they then played in people's lives. As Christopher Hill has written of the parish church in his **Reformation to Industrial Revolution**: '*It was the place where elections were held, poor relief distributed, public and private announcements made; it could be an amusement hall, a school, a library, a storehouse. In a society without radio, television and daily press, still largely illiterate and with a strict censorship (except in the revolutionary decades), the pulpit was almost the sole source of ideas on economics and politics.*'

The Great Fire of 1666

However devastating the consequences of the Fire as regards property, more importantly not a single person lost his or her life.

The major worry was that the fire would reach the White Tower which was full of gunpowder. The diarist John Evelyn estimated that if it had, the explosion '*would undoubtedly have not only beaten down and destroyed all the Bridge, but sunk and torn all the vessels in the river and rendered the demolition beyond all expression for several miles even about the country at many miles distance.*'

In fact pulling down houses halted the blaze, although it eventually reached the moat of the Tower.

The Great Fire of 1666: *Lasting for five days, the Great Fire razed to the ground the City between the Tower of London and the Temple. As always Samuel Pepys provides the human response: he buried his papers, wine and 'parmezan' cheese in the garden as a precaution.*

St. Giles Cripplegate

Cripplegate was, like Newgate and Aldgate, one of the city gates. The first church here was built in about 1090 by Alfune, the first proctor of Bart's Hospital, in honour of St. Giles, the patron saint of beggars and cripples.

Rebuilt several times in subsequent years, its splendour attracted a wide range of people, from Sir Thomas More and William Shakespeare to Ben Jonson and Oliver Crom-

Cripplegate: *One of the City gates leading towards the north. Apparently well-known for its creaky hinges, the gate was pulled down in 1760.*

well. John Milton was another regular worshipper, and on his death the blind poet was buried near the head of the central aisle, a spot marked by a tablet. Sadly, in 1790 his grave was disturbed, but the remains were eventually replaced.

Although St. Giles escaped the ravages of the Great Fire in 1666, it was not so lucky in August 1940, being hit in the first air raid on London. However it was restored, and at present sits rather forlornly in the middle of the Barbican complex.

St. Giles Cripplegate: *The names of those associated with this church are commemorated today in the neighbouring Barbican Estate: Milton Court, Cromwell Tower, and Frobisher (a great Elizabethan seaman and explorer) Crescent.*

Oliver Cromwell

Oliver Cromwell was born at Huntingdon in 1599 into a family of wealthy East Anglian landowners. As a young man he was sent to London to complete his education, probably studying law at Lincoln's Inn. In August 1620 he married Elizabeth Bourchier at St. Giles Cripplegate.

Cromwell returned to East Anglia and worked as a farmer, but the deepening struggle between Charles I and Parliament drew him into politics. He was elected an MP from 1628, first for Huntingdon and then Cambridge. By 1641 tension had reached such a point that swords were brandished on the floor of the House of Commons. In January 1642 the king entered the House of Commons to arrest five recalcitrant MPs — but to no avail as they had already fled to the safety of the City of London.

The beheading of Archbishop Laud, 1645: *Tower Hill was a prominent place of execution from the fourteenth century until 1747. Laud was beheaded for 'treason against Parliament'.*

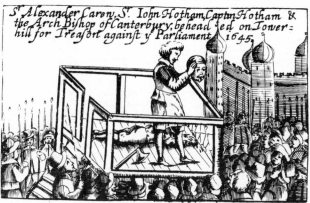

Mount Mill Fort near St. John Street: *From a contemporary account dated 9th May 1643: 'It was wonderful to see how the women and children, and vast numbers of people would come and work about, digging and carrying of earth to make their new fortifications.'*

Cromwell House, Clerkenwell: *Cromwell's memory lives on in the several Cromwell Avenues, Places and Roads.*

During the ensuing Civil War London was a stronghold of the Parliamentary forces; forts were constructed at Hyde Park Corner, Wardour Street and several other spots to guarantee its safety. 100,000 people helped to dig the trenches which stretched for nearly twenty miles around the capital. In fact the Royalists got no nearer than Brentford.

Whitehall Palace: *Charles I fled from here in 1642 because of the demonstrations led by apprentices with cropped hair — nicknamed 'roundheads'. Destroyed in a fire of 1698, only Inigo Jones' Banqueting House remains.*

Cromwell distinguished himself as a soldier by organising the New Model Army, and in 1649 he was a prime mover in the decision to execute Chares I at Whitehall. In the 1650s his influence was so powerful that he could openly dissolve a series of Parliaments at Westminster, on one occasion taking away the symbolic Mace and locking MPs out of the Chamber.

Cromwell lived in various London residences, amongst them one in Clerkenwell Close behind Clerkenwell Green, another in Drury Lane and another on the south side of Long Acre, but from 1653 when he accepted the title of Lord Protector he occupied Whitehall Palace.

Despite his rather stern image Cromwell was apparently a man of some humour — he employed four buffoons for his entertainment — and even toyed with the idea of selling off St. Paul's to the Jews as a synagogue! Cromwell was also fond of exercise, but on one occasion this liking was nearly his downfall. In September 1654 he was driving a carriage in Hyde Park when the horses bolted; Cromwell was thrown to the ground and a pistol in his pocket went off, but with only minor damage. It was also in Hyde Park that an assassin shadowed him, but no opportunity for a murder attempt presented itself.

On September 3rd, 1658, Cromwell died at Whitehall. By then he was so hated that when his body was laid in state at Somerset House in the Strand *'This folly and profusion so far provoked the people that they threw dirt in the night on his escutcheon that was placed over the great gate of Somerset House.'*

This was by no means the end of such indignities. In January 1661, after the Restoration of Charles II, Cromwell's corpse and those of two other friends were disinterred from their Westminster Abbey burial place, taken to Red Lion Square and from there to Tyburn where they were gibbetted. They were then beheaded, the bodies buried beneath the gallows and the heads placed on poles at Westminster Hall.

But reputations and memories can soon change; by July 1667 Samuel Pepys would record his discussion with an acquaintance about the respective merits of Cromwell and Charles II: *'It is strange how he and everybody else doth nowadays reflect upon Oliver and commend him so brave things he did and made all the neighbour princes fear him; while here a prince, come in with all the love and prayers and good liking of his people, and have given greater signs of loyalty and willingness to serve him with their estates than ever was done by any people, hath lost all so soon, that it is a miracle what way a man could devise to lose so much in so little time.'*

Today a three-foot-high bronze statue of Cromwell stands in New Palace Yard outside Westminster Hall.

Bronze statue of Oliver Cromwell at Westminster Hall: *Erected in 1899, the statue shows Cromwell armed with his Bible and a sword. Irish MPs refused to contribute to its cost, and the Prime Minister Lord Rosebery finally paid for it out of his own pocket.*

St. Paul's Cathedral

There have been several churches and cathedrals on the site of St. Paul's, fire having destroyed two previous buildings in 1807 and 1666. For many years it functioned as an economic and social centre. In 1554, for example, the Common Council tried to forbid *'the carrying of food'* or *'the leading of mules and horses'* through the Cathedral, but without success. Both lawyers and prostitutes took up residence behind specific pillars, and lotteries were held at the West door during Elizabethan times to raise money for the government.

Writings of the time convey the atmosphere: Thomas

Print shop at St. Paul's: *Lacking television, cinema, radio or a tabloid press, print shops functioned as a kind of early newsreel.*

Dekker in his **The Gull's Handbook** of 1609 described 'Powle's Walk' as something resembling a seventeenth-century fashion show with the tailors displaying their new creations, and John Earle testified to the continual hubbub: *'The noise in it is like that of bees, a strange humming or buzz mixed with the sound of walking feet and wagging tongues; it is a kind of still roar or loud whisper.'* The churchyard served as a place of punishment — one man found guilty of provoking a riot in the church was put in the pillory, had his ears nailed to a post and then cut off. In January 1606 four of the Gunpowder Plot conspirators were hanged, drawn and quartered before the West entrance.

During the Civil War the Puritans made a determined onslaught on what they regarded as idolatrous and papist practices. The silver vessels were sold to buy artillery, the restoration fund used to pay the Parliamentary troops, shops situated in the portico and 800 horses stabled in the nave. One contemporary royalist account regaled its readers with even worse horrors: *'they have turned it into an ale-house, a barber's shop, a smith's forge, a scullery, and, I blush to think of it, into a bawdy house.'*

Almost the whole of St. Paul's was destroyed in the Great Fire of 1666, the heat being so intense that melting lead poured down the streets in streams. The work of rebuilding it lasted from 1675 until 1710 and Sir Christopher Wren, the new cathedral's architect, had to endure endless wranglings and complications. The bulk of the money needed, approximately £750,000, came from a tax on coal.

Financial considerations preoccupied the clergy too. 'Stairsfoot' money had been charged from 1707 in order to pay for the fund set up to assist injured workmen and their families, but the fees continued long after they had left. Instead it was

39

the vergers who pocketed the money — often up to £40 per day, a considerable sum in the eighteenth century. One visitor commented on his *'pocket sweating pretty freely all the while'* and **Punch** poked fun at *'clerical showmen'*.

Nor was this the only obstacle for visitors. A committee of 1841 heard how all corners of St. Paul's were used as a public lavatory by men and women, the cathedral also being filled with *'beggars, men with burthens, women knitting, parties eating luncheon, dogs, children playing, loud laughing and talking, and every kind of scene incompatible with the solemnity of worship . . .'* Graffiti covered the walls, written by men inscribing their own *'and the names of various ladies of their acquaintance.'*

From the early nineteenth century St. Paul's was pressed into service as an appropriate showplace for the celebration of British pomp and circumstance, beginning with Nelson's state funeral in 1806, through to Queen Victoria's Diamond Jubilee in 1897 and today's royal wedding.

The Oxford Arms in 1875: *This pub in Warwick Lane dated from the seventeenth century and was an important staging post for coaches on the way to Oxford.*

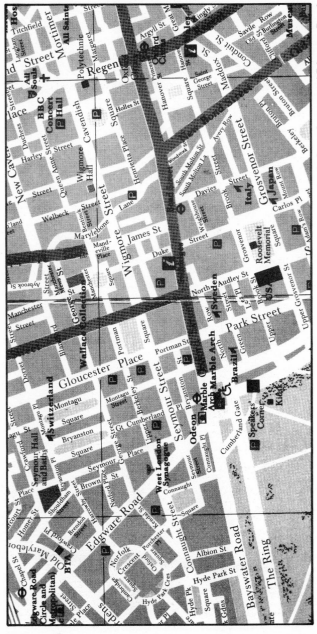

Hyde Park Corner and Edgware Road

41

Tyburn

Also known as 'Deadly Never Green', Tyburn's role as an execution place began in the Middle Ages. The gallows was originally triangular in shape, and the victims hanging from it would be in such pain that family and friends would pull down on their legs in order to speed up death.

Brought from Newgate after a three-hour cart ride through jeering crowds, the highwaymen Jack Sheppard, Jonathan Wild and John Rann were some of those despatched. Political as well as religious dissidents ended up at Tyburn, including five of the men who had signed Charles I's death warrant.

Hangings at Tyburn were something of a public holiday, London's apprentices and journeymen taking the day off to attend. 200,000 people were at Jack Sheppard's death in 1724. The novelist Henry Fielding criticised public executions: 'we sacrifice the lives of men, not for the reformation but for the diversion of the populace.' Pepys was there on January 21st, 1664, paying for a decent view: 'I got for a shilling to stand upon the wheel of a cart, in great pain, above an hour before the execution was done — he delaying the time by long discourses and prayers one after another, in hopes of a reprieve; but none came, and at last was flung off the lather in his cloak.' James Boswell saw the highwayman Paul Lewis hanged in May 1763:

The execution of 'The Idle Apprentice' at Tyburn: *Hogarth's detailed pictures vividly suggest the feel and movement of eighteenth-century London life. There is a bust of him in Leicester Square, where he lived.*

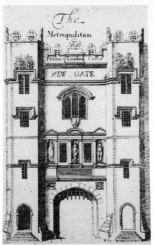

Newgate: *Incorporating a prison from the twelfth century, the gate was later rebuilt by Dick Whittington, the famous Lord Mayor of London. Like the other six city gates it was demolished in the 1760s.*

'I was most terribly shocked, and thrown into a very deep melancholy.'

By the end of the eighteenth century adjoining Mayfair had become a highly fashionable area — Tyburn Lane was renamed Park Lane — and pressure from its influential residents ensured the end of Tyburn, the last execution held in 1783. After that Newgate became the venue for these gruesome events.

All that can be seen today to mark the former location of Tyburn is a slab on a traffic island at the junction of the Bayswater-Edgware Roads near Marble Arch.

Newgate

The prison used to stand in Newgate Street, receiving its name from New Gate, the principal west gate of the City, in which it was housed during the thirteenth century.

Newgate was notorious for its squalor, overcrowding and harsh conditions. Because of the window tax the cells were airless and gloomy, the prison officials were infamous for their treatment of the inmates, and many prisoners died of gaol fever. As late as 1714 pigs could still be kept within the walls. Christopher Marlowe, Ben Jonson, Titus Oates, Daniel Defoe, William Cobbett and the two highwaymen Jonathan Wilde and Jack Sheppard were some of the well-known residents, the last managing to escape on several occasions.

The loathing with which people regarded the prison ensured that it was often attacked, as in 1381. Horace Walpole wrote to a friend in March 1752, in tones reminiscent of a stern 'law and order' enthusiast today: *'It is shocking to think what a shambles this country is grown! Seventeen were executed this morning, after having murdered the Turnkey on Friday night, and almost forced open Newgate. One is forced to travel, here at noon, as if one was going to battle.'* In 1780 Newgate Prison was razed to the ground during the Gordon Riots, but once more rebuilt.

James Boswell visited the prison, a trip which left him very depressed, as did the French woman Flora Tristan in the 1830s, who described the arsenal: *'The walls are covered with hooks on which hang every article of torture used since its foundation. They are the prison's records: massive iron collars with fetters attached, saws for hacking off limbs, racks for breaking bones, clubs, axes, swords and an assortment of instruments for extorting information from prisoners'*. By the end of her tour, she wrote *'I suffered so intensely I could hardly breathe.'*

The heads at Newgate:
Gawping at the moulded heads of executed criminals was a popular attraction at Newgate in the nineteenth century. One visitor observed that the casts were highly realistic 'with the impression of the rope clearly visible'.

Newgate Prison on execution day: *The man on the right is selling ballads and broadsides, and especially popular on occasions such as these would be the supposed 'Dying Confessions' of the condemned.*

Newgate was a prominent spot in London so it was outside the prison that Jack Cade's body was displayed in 1450, before being cut up and the quarters sent to different parts of the kingdom. With the ending of Tyburn as a place of execution in the 1780s, hangings took place here too. Crowds of up to 30,000 often began gathering the night before, and the cry of 'Hats Off!' was not a token of respect for the dead but a demand that the view should not be blocked by people in front.

Charles Dickens portrayed one such scene in **Oliver Twist**: *'A great multitude had already assembled, the windows were filled with people, smoking and playing cards to beguile the time, the crowds were pushing, quarrelling, joking. Everything told of life and animation, but one dark cluster of objects in the centre of all — the black stage, the cross-beam, the rope and all the hideous apparatus of death.'* Sometimes the corpses would be exhibited in iron cages in Newgate Street as a supposed deterrent.

The last public execution at Newgate took place in May 1868; the condemned was Michael Barrett, the ringleader of a group responsible for an explosion at the House of Detention in Clerkenwell. From then on executions were carried out within the walls, until 1902 when Newgate Prison was pulled down. In its stead rose the Old Bailey, continuity being provided by the prison stones used for the new building.

Old Bailey: *The horrible smells from nearby Newgate prison would wreak havoc at the court: in 1750 four out of six judges died, together with forty jurymen. Today's judges still carry flowers and the court is strewn with herbs as a momento of this.*

Clerkenwell Green

The area known today as Clerkenwell was famous in the Middle Ages for its springs and spas, attracting religious foundations and, later on, distilleries. At one holy well apprentices and clerks used to gather to perform mystery plays, and it was from these activities that Clerkenwell derived its name. The Clerk's Well is at 16 Farringdon Lane, now the home of the **New Statesman**.

The Green has a long history, having been used as a recreation ground by young people in the Middle Ages. In 1381 the peasants camped there, and in 1538 the chronicler Holinshed recorded its popularity as a place of execution: '*The Sunday after Barthelmew Day, was one Cratwell, hangman of London, and two persons more, hanged at the wrestling place on the backesyde of Clerkenwell besyde London, for robbying of a boothe in Bartholomew Fayre, at which execution was about twentie thousand people as I myself judged.*'

Surrounded in the seventeenth century by the houses of the prosperous — benefitting as a result of the dissolution of the monasteries — from the 1760s the Green established itself as a focus for many marches and demonstrations, or, as the **City Press** put it in 1871, '*the headquarters of republicanism, revolution and ultra non-conformity.*' John Wilkes, born a stone's throw away in St. John's Square, spoke here in 1764 and easily defeated the King's candidate for the Ward of Farringdon Without during the elections of 1768-69. William

Clerkenwell Green in 1826: *The Green was once ringed by the houses of the wealthy, but when refugees from the Great Fire stayed and put down roots the fashionable moved further westwards.*

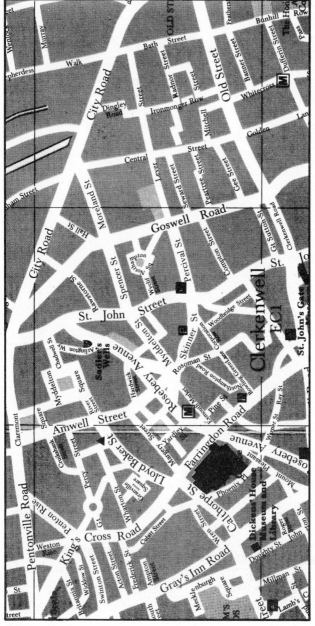

Cobbett thundered against the Corn Laws from the Green in 1826.

The large building at the bottom of the Green was once the Sessions House, constructed in 1779, the scene of many a famous trial. Here it was that in the summer of 1832 three leaders of the National Union of the Working Classes were accused of having '*with force and arms made a great riot, tumult and disturbance*'. They were acquitted by the jury, to the great joy of the huge crowd waiting outside, and chaired around the Green in triumph.

Clerkenwell Green maintained its radical reputation during the Chartist agitation of 1842 with the Prime Minister Sir Robert Peel prohibiting its use as a meeting place, and six years later the Horse Guards occupied it one night in order to forestall a planned protest. A policeman of the time, James Cornish, later recalled: '*there was plenty of open space on the Green for fighting, and many houses in which Chartists could hide and throw things at us.*'

Bigoted observers visited the Green to confirm their prejudices; the novelist George Gissing came in the late 1880s, researching his **The Nether World**: '*Last Sunday evening I spent on Clerkenwell Green — a great assembly place for radical meetings and the like. A more disturbing scene is difficult to imagine — the vulgar blatant scoundrels!*' Invariably the members of the workingmen's club at 37 Clerkenwell Green would swell the marches, and in November 1887 a large rally headed by William Morris, George Bernard Shaw and Annie Besant started from the Green for what turned out to be 'Bloody Sunday' in Trafalgar Square.

Over the years Clerkenwell Green found itself superseded by the more spacious Hyde Park as a meeting place.

Clerkenwell Green in 1900: *Clerkenwell has been for many years the home of those skilled trades concerning clocks, watches, jewellery and printing.*

John Wilkes

Born in October 1725 at St. John's Square, Clerkenwell, the son of a wealthy distiller, Wilkes was a controversial figure in his lifetime — the historian Edward Gibbon thought his conversation '*full of blasphemy and bawdy*'.

Wilkes was embroiled in politics from an early age, becoming an MP and quickly adopting a position hostile to the bribery and corruption rampant throughout Georgian England. Involved in the publication of **The North Briton**, number 45 launched a particularly vitriolic attack which prompted the government to arrest him in April 1763. Seized in his home at 13 Great George Street, Westminster, his personal belongings and papers ransacked, Wilkes was taken off to the Tower of London. Released a few days later when the judge ruled against the legality of general warrants, Wilkes returned to Great George Street to find thousands of people waiting to cheer him home.

John Wilkes: *He was well-known for his sense of humour. In 1794 crowds broke his windows at 30 Grosvenor Square in mistake for another; Wilkes shrugged aside the damage: 'They are only some of my old pupils now set up for themselves.'*

A duel in Hyde Park: *Other preferred venues for duelling were Leicester Fields — a part of which is now Leicester Square — and around Montagu House, an area where the British Museum stands today.*

In November 1763 Wilkes fought a duel after he had called a certain Samuel Martin a *'low fellow and dirty tool of power'*. Martin was in the pay of the government and had been practising his shooting for some months; when they fought near the Ring in Hyde Park, Wilkes was badly wounded in the stomach. He slowly recovered, but decided that it would be wise to leave England for a while.

On his return in 1768 he was involved in a series of bitterly contested elections, popular support for him evidenced by the way the number '45' appeared everywhere — the Austrian ambassador was even held upside down while '45' was chalked on the soles of his boots! Although Wilkes won his second election, he still had to serve a spell of imprisonment in the King's Bench Prison for libel and obscenity. Whilst there he was four times expelled from the House of Commons and four times re-elected as the Member for Middlesex. Wilkes was also elected Alderman for the Ward of Farringdon Without in January 1769.

On his release from the King's Bench Prison in April 1770 he jumped straight back into the fray, eventually securing the right that parliamentary proceedings could be legally reported. Wilkes was a fervent supporter of the American Revolution and in 1776 unsuccessfully proposed a Bill *'for a just and equal representation of the people of England in Parliament'* — more than fifty years before the first Reform Act was passed in 1832. In 1780 the Gordon Riots, which began as an anti-Catholic outburst, turned into a general attack on property — Dickens provides a lurid picture in **Barnaby Rudge** — and Wilkes as a powerful city figure was called upon to re-assert law and order. When the crowd threatened the Bank of England Wilkes commanded the troops to open fire, an action which ended his popular appeal.

The rest of his life was spent quietly. His marriage had not been a success, but he was very attached to his daughter Polly and they lived together at 30 Grosvenor Square, on the corner of South Audley Street, from 1789. He died there in December 1797 and was buried in the vaults beneath nearby Grosvenor Chapel where he had been a frequent worshipper. There is a marble tablet on the east wall which commemorates 'A Friend to Liberty'.

Westminster Election of 1780: *Lasting over two weeks, the elections were violent and bloody contests. One late eighteenth-century observer complained that the 'vulgar abuse of the candidates from the vilest rabble is not rendered endurable by either wit or good temper.'*

The Gordon Riots of 1780: *'£100,000 of damage was done to property (ten times as much as in Paris throughout the French Revolution) before troops restored order at the cost of 290 citizens' lives: twenty-five looters were later executed.'* — Roy Porter 'English Society in the Eighteenth Century' (1982).

Kemble faces the 'Old Prices' rioters: *There were 'OP' dances, badges, hats, umbrellas and even 'OP' toothpicks. When Kemble finally apologised, a placard was hoisted in the auditorium which read 'We Are Satisfied'. Note the spikes at the front of the stage.*

Covent Garden Theatre

The first theatre was built on this site in 1732, and together with the neighbouring Theatre Royal in Drury Lane they were the only such dramatic establishments allowed in London, legally at least, until 1843.

In 1808 the theatre was burnt down and its lavish successor, rebuilt at a cost of £300,000, was opened the following year with increased admission prices. As the proprietor, John Philip Kemble, stepped forward to deliver the opening address he was greeted by a tumult of groans, hisses, cat-calls, curses and shouts of 'Old Prices'.

These, the 'Old Price Riots', lasted for sixty-six consecutive nights as Kemble insisted that the play should still be performed — even though no one could hear a word — whilst the audience turned the theatre into a gigantic fairground with an orgy of noise, dancing and singing; sometimes pigs and pigeons were released into the auditorium! One commentator, Leigh Hunt, observed that *'the actors had become the audience, and the audience the actors.'* Eventually Kemble had to back down and apologise to the spectators.

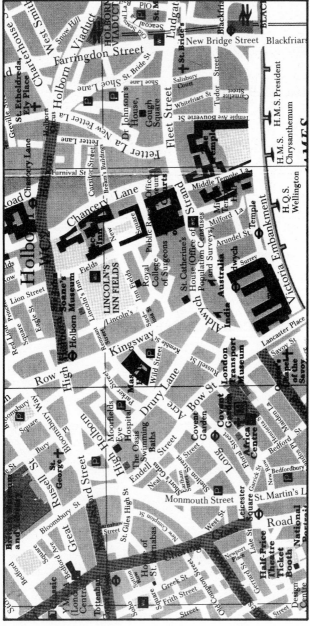

Covent Garden and St. Giles

In the first half of the nineteenth century theatres were surrounded by swarms of prostitutes, often young women who had migrated from the country and were unable to find work. One newspaper in the 1840s referred to the Covent Garden and Drury Lane theatres as *'great public brothels'*. Burnt down once again in 1856, within two years it was opened as, and still is, the Royal Opera House, Covent Garden.

Royal Opera House, Covent Garden in the 1950s: *There has been a theatre on this site since 1732. When it burnt down in 1808 23 firemen died and Handel's organ and the scores of some of his operas were destroyed. The designer of the present building was Sir Edward Barry.*

Covent Garden market: *'From Long Acre to the Strand on the one side, and from Bow-street to Bedford-street on the other, the ground has been seized upon by the market-goers.'* — Henry Mayhew 'London Labour and the London Poor' (1861).

The Cato Street Conspiracy

Severe unemployment and poverty marked the ending of the Napoleonic wars in a country already wracked by the onset of industrialisation and the rapid growth of towns and cities. London, for example, grew from just under a million inhabitants in 1800 to four and a half million in 1900.

A number of fringe organisations plotted with varying degrees of seriousness to overthrow the government, their memberships riddled with spies and *agents provocateur*. In February 1820 Arthur Thistlewood and some associates drew up plans to assassinate the Cabinet, including the Duke of Wellington, whilst they were dining with the Earl of Harrowby at his residence in 39 Grosvenor Square.

The conspirators met above a stable at 1a Cato Street, just off the Edgware Road, and were finalising the arrangements on 23rd February — the evening of the intended assassination — when they were surprised by the arrival of the Bow Street Runners (the forerunners of the Metropolitan Police, not introduced until 1829). Of those captured, five including Thistlewood were hanged outside Newgate and four transported.

The building in Cato Street remains almost unaltered to this day and a GLC blue plaque is visible on its side.

The end of the Cato Street Conspiracy: *One of the conspirators was William Davidson, probably the first coloured person to play a significant part in British politics. He was hanged together with the others on 1st May 1820.*

Karl and Jenny Marx

Karl Marx arrived in London in August 1849 after he had been expelled from a number of other European countries. It was a London crowded with two and a half million people and marked by the most bitter inequalities. Frederick Engels wrote a scathing description of the metropolis in 1844: '*The very turmoil of the streets has something against which human nature rebels. Hundreds of thousands crowd by one another as though they had nothing in common, it occurs to no man to honour another with so much as a glance.*'

Marx had been to London before 1849 to deliver lectures, but this time he stayed until his death in March 1883, grappling with the many problems of exile life. As his fellow *émigré* William Liebknecht later commented: '*In London it was extremely difficult to obtain a secure livelihood, and the hunger drove most of the fugitives into the country or to America . . .*'

When his wife Jenny and three children joined him, the family found lodgings in Chelsea at 4 Anderson Street. But in April 1850 the Marxes, unable to pay the rent, were evicted and had to take temporary accommodation at the German Hotel, 1-2 Leicester Street, off Leicester Square (now a smart restaurant). In May 1850 they moved to 64 Dean Street, Soho (since demolished) and then to two rooms at 28 Dean Street, where they lived for six years until September 1856 (the building still stands, with a GLC plaque on the wall).

It was here that the Marxes experienced the most abject poverty. Their rooms on the first floor had to accommodate Karl, Jenny, their maid Lenchen and a growing family. Three of their children died at 28 Dean Street — on one occasion the penniless Marx had to beg for money to buy a coffin for the

Rookeries of St. Giles: *Lord Byron speaking in the House of Lords, 1812: 'I have been in some of the most oppressed provinces of Turkey, but never, under the most despotic of infidel governments, did I behold such squalid wretchedness as I have seen since my return, in the very heart of a Christian country.'*

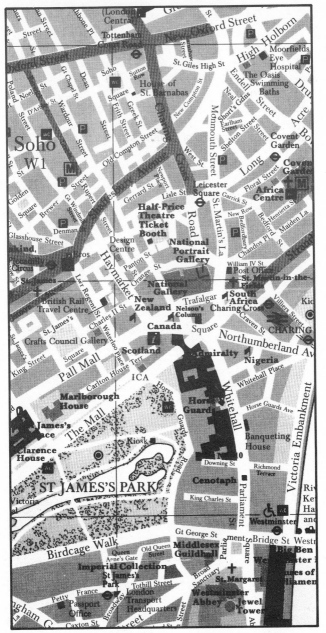

Soho to Trafalgar Square

Karl Marx: *Daughter Eleanor later wrote of her parents: 'Assuredly two people never enjoyed a joke more than these two. Again and again — especially if the occasion were one demanding decorum and sedateness, have I seen them laugh till tears ran down their cheeks.'*

28 Dean Street: *During the six years that Marx lived here he wrote most of 'Capital'. Dean Street, built in the 1680s, had long been a haunt for artists and immigrants.*

dead Franziska.

Yet however appalling the conditions Karl and Jenny tried to create a warm and friendly domestic atmosphere, as a Prussian spy who kept watch on them noted: *'in the apartment there is not one clean and good piece of furniture to be found: all is broken, tattered and torn, everywhere clings thick dust, everywhere is in the greatest disorder . . . But all this gives Marx and his wife not the slightest embarrassment; one is received in the friendliest way.'*

Marx worked hard at the nearby British Museum — *'where I am most often from 9 in the morning until 7 in the evening'* — but he always retained his sense of fun, and everyone testifies to the lively Sunday outings spent on Hampstead Heath as family and friends polished off a hamper and played games with the children. Marx used to frequent a 'sword room' off

9 (later 46) Grafton Terrace: *Jenny Marx: 'it was like a palace for us in comparison with the places we had lived in before'; although it 'was not easy to get to.'*

41 Maitland Park Road: *Engels lived nearby at 122 Regent's Park Road from 1870-1894, and he and Marx would often go for a stroll together on Hampstead Heath.*

Oxford Street, loved walking and knew London intimately — something which served him well during a pub crawl down Tottenham Court Road. After leaving the eighteenth Marx and his companions shattered some streetlamps with a volley of stones, and found themselves being chased by four policemen. In the words of Liebknecht: *'Marx showed a turn of speed that I should not have attributed to him. And after the wild chase had lasted some minutes, we succeeded in turning into a side street and there running through an alley . . . whence we came behind the policemen who lost the trail.'*

In September 1856 the family moved to 9 Grafton Terrace, Fitzroy Road, a house which Jenny called 'princely' in comparison to Dean Street. Renumbered 46 and still standing, they stayed there until March 1864 when they moved to 1 Maitland Park Road — here Marx was summoned for the non-payment of his rates in 1868 — and to no. 41 in 1875 (bombed in the Blitz and later demolished). Both Jenny and Karl died at 41 Maitland Park Road, and on March 17th 1883 he was buried at Highgate Cemetery in the same grave as his wife and daughter.

Hyde Park

Hyde Park is still the largest open space in London, amounting in all to some 360 acres. The land originally belonged to the Church of Westminster until Henry VIII appropriated it in 1536 to hunt hare and pheasant for his own amusement. The Park was opened to the public under the Stuarts and became famous for its running and horse races.

The Parliamentary forces built a camp in it during the Civil War and later sold it off to private purchasers. The diarist John Evelyn recorded his indignation in an entry for April 11th, 1653: *'I went to take the aire in Hide Park, where every coach was made to pay a shilling, and horse 6d, by the sordid fellow who had purchased it of the State as they were cal'd.'*

After the Restoration, Charles II cancelled the sale of Hyde Park and in 1662 it was once more made available to the public. It soon established a reputation as a haunt for highwaymen. Innocent parties crossing the Park at night would gather in groups, hoping for safety in numbers, but often the robbers preferred to work in broad daylight. Hyde Park also hosted a fashion parade — Pepys wrote of meeting the Duke of York *'who did eye my wife mightily'* — and some observers counted a thousand coaches an evening perambulating around Rotten Row.

In the eighteenth century Hyde Park was a notorious place for duels: 172 were fought between 1760 and 1820, one of them involving John Wilkes. Henry Fielding in his novel **Amelia**

Hyde Park Corner in 1750: *Hyde Park Corner today is a fearsome roundabout congested with cars and lorries, and the contrast with the picture below brings out the accelerating pace of London life.*

of 1751 referred to it as: *'that place, which may be properly called the field of blood, being that part a little to the left of The Ring, which heroes have chosen for their exit out of this world.'*

During the nineteenth century the Park acquired fame as the venue for many political marches and demonstrations. In July 1866 a meeting organised by the Reform League was to be held at the Park to demand an extension of the right to vote, but the Home Secretary and Commissioner of Police decided it should not be allowed and ordered the gates to be locked. When the crowd, estimated at between one hundred and two hundred thousand, discovered this they tore down half a mile of railings and went ahead with the meeting. Karl Marx summed up the incident: *'If the railings — and it was touch and go — had been used offensively and defensively against the police and about twenty had been knocked dead, the military would have had to "intervene" instead of only parading.*

The Hyde Park Riots of July 1866: *The government had taken the most elaborate precautions, drafting in nearly 2000 policemen and five companies of Coldstream Guards. To no avail, as an eyewitness recalled: 'They belaboured the front rank with their batons, but were swept aside like flies before the waiter's napkin.'*

Pulling down the railings at Hyde Park, 1866: *The Liberal Prime Minister William Gladstone once noted: 'I am sorry to say that if no instructions had been addressed in political crises to the people of this country except to remember to hate violence, to love order and to exercise patience, the liberties of this country would never have been attained.'*

61

Strike-bound buses in Hyde Park, 1926: *In May 1926 the trade union movement struck in support of the miners. The TUC called off the action after nine days.*

And then there would have been some fun.' The pressure of such incidents finally brought about the Reform Act of 1867.

In 1890 Hyde Park witnessed the first May Day celebrations held in this country. The impetus came from the campaign for the eight-hour day and caught the imagination of the capital. Up to half a million people marched to the Park and, as the **Star** put it, *'It seemed as though the whole population of London poured parkwards . . .'*

Hyde Park was used as a government munitions store throughout the nineteenth century, and during the General Strike of 1926 food dumps were set up and troops drilled

The Hunger Marchers at Hyde Park in 1932: *The Hunger Marchers were protesting about mass unemployment and the degrading means test which split up families.*

there in preparation. In the 1930s it was once more the reception point for a number of marches — in this case the Hunger Marchers of 1932, 1934 and 1936 when unemployed men and women marched to London to publicise their plight. In 1932, when Londoners assembled to meet the marchers, mounted police cleared the Park with baton charges, a tactic prevented four years later when a huge crowd of 250,000 gathered. In September 1934 Oswald Mosley and his British Union of Fascists tried to hold a meeting, but the noise of the counter-demonstration drowned their proceedings. During the Blitz shelters were dug in the Park and buses parked under the trees at night.

One attraction of Hyde Park has always been Speakers' Corner, where a variety of soap-box orators try to put the world to rights. William Morris and Lenin were just two of the well-known figures who visited it. Some of the speakers established formidable reputations, and the ferment of debate and heckling has even been called a 'People's University.' From time to time there have been attempts to restrict the selling of literature — Orwell attacked the arrest of five sellers in December 1945 and called the meetings: '*one of the minor wonders of the world ... Granted that Hyde Park is a special area, a sort of Alsatia where outlawed opinions were permitted to walk — still, there are very few countries in the world where you can see a similar spectacle.*'

Speakers' Corner in 1965: *Marble Arch in the background was moved to its present site in 1851. Once outside Buckingham Palace, it was found to be too small for the state coaches to get through and was pensioned off.*

Highgate Cemetery

A decent burial for the dead was one facility in which Londoners appeared to have shown little interest, especially at times of plague. During the Black Death of 1348, 50,000 victims were heaped together at Charterhouse — the spot where later the priory and public school were situated. In the Great Plague of 1665 the corpses were interred in mass graves, as Daniel Defoe described in his **A Journal of the Plague Year**: *'They died by heaps, and they were buried by heaps.'*

But with the rapid expansion of London's population at the beginning of the nineteenth century, city churchyards and other burial sites were full to bursting. Many of them were closed and converted to recreation areas: such was the case with Spa Fields in Clerkenwell, opened in 1886. Local authorities showed little concern, so it was left to private companies to sell graves in their own newly-built cemeteries. The cemetery at Kensal Green opened in 1833, at Norwood in 1838 and Highgate in 1838 — just some of the 70 new cemeteries constructed in London by the end of the nineteenth century. Highgate cemetery proved so profitable that an extension on the east side of Swains Lane was opened in 1856.

Many famous and not so famous people ended up at Highgate. In the Western cemetery, for instance, you can find John Atcheler, horse-slaughterer to Queen Victoria; but also the graves of Jacob Bronowski, Charles Dickens' wife and daughter, Michael Faraday and the Rossetti family. In the Eastern cemetery there are George Eliot, the Chartist G.J.

Death in London: *An experience with which Londoners were all too familiar; as late as the eighteenth century three-quarters of the capital's children failed to reach the age of five.*

Holyoake, and the philosophers George Henry Lewes and Herbert Spencer. Unfortunately subsequent neglect of the cemetery was such that of the 51,000 graves containing about 166,000 bodies, few can be identified — in particular, most of the 'common' graves of the nineteenth century have long since disappeared.

Probably the best known tomb at Highgate is that of Karl Marx, which lies in the unconsecrated ground of the Eastern cemetery. He was buried in the same grave as his wife Jenny. In 1898 their daughter Eleanor, a noted socialist who had played a prominent role in the dock strike of 1889, was buried at the same spot. In 1954 their bodies were moved a hundred years to a less crowded location (although a tablet marks the original memorial) and two years later Lawrence Bradshaw sculpted a new bust of Marx which now stands on a base carrying the slogan 'Workers of All Lands Unite'.

Today the Western cemetery remains permanently closed except for specified days, but the Eastern cemetery is open to visitors. A voluntary organisation, the Friends of Highgate Cemetery, has been trying to rescue the cemetery from the dilapidation it has suffered in recent years.

Marx's tomb in Highgate Cemetery: *Often defaced and daubed with paint, a few years ago an attempt was made to blow it up with explosives. Every year on March 14th a short ceremony is held here, organised by the Marx Memorial Library.*

The western part of Highgate Cemetery: *The designer of the cemetery, Stephen Geary, is himself buried here, and the grandeur of his plan is evidenced by the Egyptian columns, Egyptian Avenue and the Cedar of Lebanon Catacombs.*

William Morris

William Morris was born at Walthamstow on 24th March 1834, the son of a wealthy businessman. Between 1848 and 1856 he lived at Water House, Walthamstow — now the home of the William Morris Gallery which opened in 1950.

On coming down from Oxford Morris lived with his friend Edward Burne-Jones at 17 Red Lion Square — a plaque outside also commemorates the poet and painter Rossetti who lived there in 1851. Morris was well-known for his fiery temper, leading to many skirmishes with their maid nick-named 'Red Lion Mary'. However it was Mary who came to the rescue whenever they had hordes of people to stay, as Burne-Jones' future wife recalled: *'She cheerfully spread mattresses on the floor for friends who stayed there, and when the mattresses came to an end it was said that she built up beds with boots and portmanteaux.'*

Whilst at no. 17 Morris began designing and producing household goods with his friend Philip Webb, and in April 1861 he set up the firm of Morris and Co., which included a workshop and showroom, at 8 Red Lion Square (no longer standing). As the firm became increasingly successful in the

17 Red Lion Square: *William Morris and his great friend Edward Burne-Jones paid rent of £1 a week for 3 rooms on the 1st floor; the artist Rossetti had lived here in 1851.*

William Morris: *A man of tremendous energy and dynamism; he wrote in a letter of August 1881: 'To do nothing but grumble and not to act — that is throwing away one's life.'*

'Bloody Sunday' in Trafalgar Square, November 1887: *'all the arms collected from that vast crowd amounted to three pokers, one piece of wood, and an oyster knife.' (R.B. Cunninghame Graham)*

fields of furniture production, stained glass design, wallpapers and textiles, the Red Lion Square office proved too small so it was moved to 26 Queen's Square, Bloomsbury, where Morris and his family lived from 1865 to 1872.

A man of huge talent, whether as a designer or poet, Morris immersed himself in active politics from the mid-1870s. He supported the Twentieth Century Press at 37a Clerkenwell Green by guaranteeing the first year's rent, and in November 1887 he spoke on the Green and then led a section of 6,000 people to a rally in Trafalgar Square. Attacked by the police in St. Martin's Lane, Morris managed

The coach house at Kelmscott House: *Morris had this converted into a lecture room. Some of those who attended the meetings and the Sunday evening suppers which followed were George Bernard Shaw and W.B. Yeats.*

to make his way to the Square where similar violent scenes were being enacted. R.B. Cunninghame Graham later wrote of 'Bloody Sunday': '*The tops of the houses and hotels were crowded with well-dressed women, who clapped their hands when some miserable and half-starved working man was knocked down and trodden under foot.*'

Morris also took part in various political activities at Hyde Park; in July 1884 on his way to a meeting in favour of extending the vote he encountered a familiar problem: '*We found it easy work getting rid of the gratis literature but hard to sell anything.*' On June 12th 1886, he spoke at Speakers' Corner, writing to his daughter Jenny: '*I was quite nervous about it, I don't know why . . . I spoke twice, the second time not at all nervously.*' In July of that year he was arrested for obstructing the highway at Bell Street, off the Edgware Road, and fined a shilling and costs.

Although Morris lived at various times in two beautiful houses outside London, the Red House at Bexleyheath and Kelmscott Manor in Gloucestershire, he remained at heart a Londoner, writing in a letter: '*I rather want to be in London again, for I feel as if my time were passing with too little done in the country; altogether I fear I am a London bird; its soot has been rubbed into me, and even these autumn mornings can't wash me clean of restlessness.*'

From 1878 until his death in October 1896 Morris lived at Kelmscott House in Hammersmith. Meetings of the Hammersmith Socialist Society were frequently held in the coach house Morris had converted into a lecture room.

Lenin

Almost all the Bolshevik leaders spent some time in London at the beginning of this century, unable to organise in Czarist Russia without attracting the attention of the secret police.

One of the exiles, Ivan Maisky, described in his autobiography **Journey into the Past** the feeling of isolation that the immensity of London induced in most émigrés, especially when compared with that other centre of exile life, Paris: '*London was a leviathan, not only by virtue of its vast population but for sheer size. When I was living there the population was double that of Paris and the area it occupied at least three or four times bigger than the area of the French capital . . . Four to five thousand Russian exiles were just lost in this giant human anthill.*'

Lenin arrived in London with his wife Krupskaya in April 1902, renting two unfurnished rooms at 30 Holford Square

Lenin: *The writer Arthur Ransome met him in 1919: 'More than ever, Lenin struck me as a happy man. Walking home from the Kremlin, I tried to think of any other man of his calibre who had a similar joyous temperament. I could think of none.'*

Holford Square: *Staying at number 30 between 1902-03, Lenin found the atmosphere so oppressive that he was glad to sneak away and spend days immersed in the wealth of material at the British Museum.*

'Justice': Published between 1884-1925, 'Justice' was one of the most influential journals of the British Left. For most of that time it was issued from 37 Clerkenwell Green.

'Iskra': The little room at 37 Clerkenwell Green where Harry Quelch worked on 'Justice' and Lenin on 'Iskra' was so small that, in Lenin's words, 'there was no room for another chair.'

off Great Percy Street in King's Cross Road — the start of the first and longest of his six visits to Britain. The landlady was worried by 'Mrs Richter's' lack of a wedding ring and her disinterest in the kitchen, but finally reassured by Krupskaya's liking for Mrs Yeo's cat. Holford Square was bombed out of existence in 1940.

Throwing himself into London life, Lenin obtained a Reader's ticket for the British Museum — he supposedly sat at L13 — and explored the capital by long rides on the top of omnibuses, by bicycle and on foot. The couple also visited Primrose Hill and Marx's grave at Highgate Cemetery, as well as entertaining political visitors — Trotsky met Lenin in October 1902 at Holford Square.

Lenin and Krupskaya were anxious to improve their English, which they did by spending time at Speakers' Corner: 'We stood in the front row and carefully studied the orator's mouth. We went fairly often to Hyde Park, where speakers harangued the passing crowds on diverse themes. An atheist, standing among a group of curious listeners, proved there was no God. We were particularly keen on listening to one speaker of this kind. He spoke with an Irish accent, which was easier for us *to understand.*' Lenin with an Irish accent?

The Bolshevik paper **Iskra** was an integral part of their propaganda, and Lenin seized upon the Twentieth Century Press at 37 Clerkenwell Green as a suitable location for printing it. Between 1902-03 numbers 22 to 38 were set into type at a little printers in the East End and then run off at Clerkenwell Green. Lenin shared the editorial office with Harry Quelch, manager of the press and editor of the weekly **Justice**. In May 1903 Lenin spoke at an Alexandra Palace demonstration celebrating May Day before leaving for Geneva a few days later.

Lenin returned to London on a number of occasions. In April 1905 he came for the 3rd Congress of the Russian Social-Democratic Party, staying at 16 Percy Circus. A plaque was erected here in 1962 but the house was knocked down seven years later — a commemorative plaque can now be seen at the rear of the Royal Scot Hotel near by. In 1907 Lenin returned for the 5th Congress and in May 1908 he spent a month researching at the British Museum. In November 1911 he was Mr Ouliaff at 6 Oakley Square, off Crowndale Road, NW1.

There were three Congresses of the Russian Social-Democratic Party held in London, but the whereabouts of those held in 1903 and 1905 is uncertain. In May 1907, with the 330 delegates (who included Stalin and Trotsky) shadowed by police, the Congress took place at the Brotherhood Church in Southgate Road, Islington. The Church was on the corner of Balmes Road but was demolished about 1930; its site is now occupied by a factory.

The Crown and Woolpack, St. John Street: *Built in 1797, Lenin is supposed to have addressed a political meeting here. Pubs often provided convenient venues, another famous one being the White Hart in Drury Lane — there has been a pub on this site since 1216.*

Marx Memorial Library: *The Library stands on the land of what was once the medieval nunnery of St. Mary. The building dates from the 1730s when it was founded as a Welsh Charity School. The church of St. James stands in the background.*

37a Clerkenwell Green

Built as a Welsh Charity School in 1738 for the children of families who had emigrated from Wales, 37a Clerkenwell Green was used in turn as a coffee room, a chemist, a grocers and a pub after the school left in the 1770s.

No doubt influenced by the political sympathies of Clerkenwell's skilled craftsmen and the Green's radical reputation, a republican club called the London Patriotic Club moved into 37 Clerkenwell Green in 1872. Its initial subscribers included John Stuart Mill and the old Chartist and newspaper editor George Reynolds. Workingmen's clubs were mushrooming all over London at this time — 245 such clubs had affiliated to the central union in 1873 — and they offered members a chance to relax, to have a drink, read the newspapers and take part in a Sunday evening meeting and debate. Some clubs were more political than others and the London Patriotic Club, open from the first to women, was immersed in contemporary affairs.

In 1893 the Club moved out, to be replaced by the socialist Twentieth Century Press, an organisation responsible for the weekly paper **Justice** and a wide range of other publications, from children's stories and leaflets to Walter Crane's **Cartoons for the Cause**.

The Twentieth Century Press went into a steep decline during the First World War, reflecting the severe divisions within the labour movement regarding the war, and in 1922 moved to Southwark; once again the building was divided and used by a variety of businesses.

In 1933 a conference was organised to commemorate the 50th anniversary of Karl Marx's death, and, as a response to the book burnings then taking place in Nazi Germany, it was decided to establish a library. The Marx Memorial Library and Workers' School opened in October of that year.

Damaged by bombs during the Blitz, the Library briefly moved to 1 Doughty Street before returning in 1946. Now well established as a reference and lending library with a collection of over 100,000 books, pamphlets, newspapers and photographs, it also houses the J.D. Bernal Peace Library,

International Brigade Archive and the James Klugmann Collection, an outstanding library of chartist and radical literature. Lectures and classes are also held, and downstairs in the meeting hall hangs a banner made by William Morris for the Hammersmith Socialist Society.

Oxford Street

Originally called 'The Way to Uxbridge' it later became known as Tyburn Road and established an unsavory reputation for itself, one eighteenth-century observer referred to it as 'the lurking Place of cut-throats'.

By the early 1700s the area was gradually becoming more respectable and the road was renamed Oxford Street after

The Court of King Cholera: *There were still cholera epidemics as late as 1866-67. The 'Two Londons' of rich and poor existed side by side until the second half of the nineteenth century when many slums and cellars were demolished and their dwellers driven into the East End.*

Swan and Edgar's after Suffragette stone-throwing in 1912: *This was a fashionable drapers on the corner of Piccadilly Circus. The name comes from 'pikadille', a form of seventeenth-century neckware.*

Robert Harley, 1st earl of Oxford. With the development of shopping it expanded its activities; a German visitor of 1786 noted that the shops stayed open until 10 o'clock in the evening. By the late nineteenth century Oxford Street was attracting a rash of big department stores — from Marshall and Snellgrove in 1870, Selfridge's in 1914 and John Lewis rebuilt in 1939.

In 1908 and 1909 the Suffragettes embarked upon a campaign of assaults on property, breaking windows in Oxford Circus and Bond Street with the kind of effects graphically conveyed by the **Daily Mail**: *'From every part of the crowded and brilliantly lighted streets came the crash of splintered glass. People started as windows shattered at their side; suddenly there was another crash in front of them; on the other side of the street; behind — everywhere.'*

Today Oxford Street is a rather more sedate, and very busy, shopping centre.

Procession of Suffragettes in Piccadilly following the body of Emily Davison: *During Derby Day at Epsom in 1913 Emily Davison had thrown herself in front of the King's horse and was killed. It was one of the most dramatic attempts to publicise the 'Votes for Women' campaign.*

The Blitz

Having failed to gain control of the air during the 'Battle of Britain', Hitler's strategy to defeat Britain during the Second World War was changed to an attempt to undermine morale by bombing towns and cities.

The first bombs fell by mistake on London on August 24th 1940, but the Blitz did not start until September 7th: the beginning of 76 consecutive nights of bombing. On December 29th there was the 'Second Fire of London' with over 1400 fires in the City alone. Although Westminster Abbey, the Tower of London and the British Museum were damaged in the Blitz, St. Paul's survived intact. Luckily an unexploded bomb found near its foundations was successfully prised out and detonated in Hackney Marshes. Between September 1940 and May 1941 nearly 20,000 tons of bombs were dropped on London, killing about 30,000 people and totally destroying 220,000 homes.

At first the authorities, slow in providing shelters, were against people using underground stations but could not prevent anyone simply buying a ticket and taking up a spot.

Oxford Street in 1941: *Despite much loss of life and widespread destruction, London could and did survive the Blitz. 'It demonstrated how ordinary people could carry on.' — Tom Harrisson 'Living Through the Blitz' (1978).*

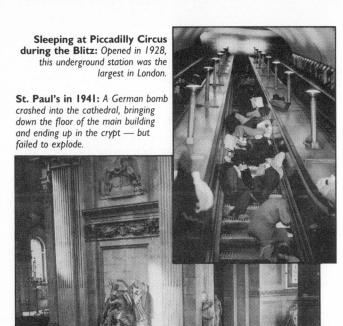

Sleeping at Piccadilly Circus during the Blitz: *Opened in 1928, this underground station was the largest in London.*

St. Paul's in 1941: *A German bomb crashed into the cathedral, bringing down the floor of the main building and ending up in the crypt — but failed to explode.*

Many of these shelters evolved a communal and social life with singing, drama, darts and other forms of entertainment. The Swiss Cottage contingent, numbering over 1,500, even produced their own magazine. Unfortunately both the Marble Arch and Bank stations received direct hits.

At its peak some 180,000 people slept underground, the majority staying either in their homes, going to other shelters such as those in the East End docks, or trekking out to Epping Forest.

Afterword

The lasting impression left behind by these pages is that of the resilience of London and its people, the refusal simply to lie down and give in.

From the mood of truculence recognised by William the Conqueror; the hostility towards kings displayed in the Middle Ages and then again in the Civil War; the support given to 'Wilkes and Liberty'; its place as a sanctuary for exiles and refugees; the welcome for the Hunger Marchers in the 1930s; the courage demonstrated in the Blitz — Londoners have never been slow in expressing a proud independence as well as a sense of community remarkable in such an enormous city.

Froissart's comments on the obstinate and presumptuous Londoners, quoted at the front of this book, were in fact written during the fourteenth century — but they apply just as well to later experiences like the Blitz. It is a spirit which although sometimes hidden never dies out, and it is something that Britain's rulers ignore at their peril.

Trafalgar Square: *Every year about twenty-five organisations apply for permission to hold demonstrations in the Square — and since 1979 the largest have been held by CND.*

Further reading

There have been literally thousands of books published about London. The following list indicates those I found most helpful, but the best way to get to know the city is on foot. Many of the places covered in this book produce useful guidelines and other material.

General and Reference
(place of publication London unless stated)

R.D. Altick *The Shows of London* (Harvard, 1978); F.R. Banks *The New Penguin Guide to London* (1982); Felix Barker and Peter Jackson *London* (1980); Charles Poulsen *The English Rebels* (1984); S.E. Rasmussen *London: the Unique City* (1982); Edgell Rickword and Jack Lindsay *Spokesmen for Liberty* (1941); Ben Weinreb and Christopher Hibbert *The London Encyclopaedia* (1983); H. Wheatley and P. Cunningham *London Past and Present* (3 volumes, 1891).

The Beginnings

W. Benham and C. Welch *Mediaeval London* (1911); Gordon Home *Roman London* (1948).

The Middle Ages

L. Butler *The Order of St. John and the Peasants' Revolt* (1982); J. Clayton *The True Story of Jack Cade* (1909); Alec Forshaw *Smithfield Past and Present* (1980); G. Kriehn *The English Rising in 1450* (Strasburg, 1892); Henry Morley *Memoirs of Bartholomew Fair* (1857); A.L. Morton *When the People Arose* (1981).

The Seventeenth and Eighteenth Centuries

James Boswell *The London Journal* (1950); John Buchan *Oliver Cromwell* (1934); D. George *London Life in the Eighteenth Century* (1951); J. Hawkes (ed) *The London Journal of Flora Tristan* (1982); R. Latham (ed) *The Illustrated Pepys* (1982); A. Rothstein *A House on Clerkenwell Green* (1983); O.A. Sherrard *A Life of John Wilkes* (1930); Audrey Williamson *Wilkes, A Friend to Liberty* (1974).

The Nineteenth Century

Asa Briggs *Marx in London* (1982); Philip Henderson (ed) *The Letters of William Morris* (1950); Wilhelm Liebknecht *Biographical Memoirs* (1975); Jack Lindsay *William Morris* (1975); *Reminiscences of Marx and Engels* (Moscow, no date).

The Twentieth Century

Angus Calder *The People's War* (1969); Dorothy Davis *A History of Shopping* (1966); N. Krupskaya *Memories of Lenin* (1970); Ivan Maisky *Journey into the Past* (1962); A. Rothstein *Lenin in Britain* (1970).

Opening times of places mentioned

Banqueting House, Whitehall: weekdays 10-5, Sunday 2-5.

British Museum: weekdays 10-5, Sunday 2.30-6.

Central Criminal Court (Old Bailey): Saturdays at 11, weekdays at 11 and 3 (when the court is not sitting); a small number of spectators are allowed in the public galleries when the court is in session.

City Records Office, Guildhall: Monday-Friday 9.30-5.

Clerk's Well: Phone Finsbury Public Library (01-609 3051 Ext 65) for appointment.

Dickens House, 48 Doughty Street: weekdays 10-5.

Guildhall: admission to the Court of Common Council every 3rd Thursday in the month 1pm. The Guildhall Museum is now housed at the Museum of London.

Highgate Cemetery: Eastern part weekdays 9-4, Sunday 12-4; Western part by appointment.

Houses of Parliament: Saturdays, Easter and Spring Bank Holiday Mondays and Tuesdays, each Monday, Tuesday and Thursday in August, and each Thursday in September 10-5.

Marx Memorial Library: Monday and Friday 2-6, Tuesday, Wednesday and Thursday 2-9, Saturday 11-1.

William Morris Gallery, Walthamstow: Tuesday-Saturday 10-1, 2-5, 1st Sunday in month 10-12, 2-5.

Museum of London: Tuesday-Saturday 10-6, Sunday 2-6.

St. Bartholomew the Great: Daily from 7.45 am to dusk.

St. Giles Cripplegate: Monday-Friday 9.30-2, Sunday 7.45-12 and 2.30-5.

St. John's Gate and Museum: Tuesday, Friday and Saturday 10-6 (guided tours at 11 and 2.30).

St. Mary-le-Bow: Monday-Friday 9.30-2, Sunday 7.45-12 and 2.30-5.

St. Paul's Cathedral: weekdays 8-7, Sundays 8-6 (5 October-March).

Savoy Chapel: Tuesday-Friday 11.30-3.30 (closed August and September).

Tower of London: weekdays 9.30-5 (March-October) or 9.30-4 (November-February), Sundays 2-5 (March-October only).

Westminster Abbey: daily 8-6 (to 8 on Wednesdays), Sundays only nave and aisles open.

Name index

(The index covers both text references and captions to illustrations; **bold** page numbers indicate detailed passages.)

Place index

(The index covers both text references and captions to illustrations; **bold** page numbers indicate detailed passages.)

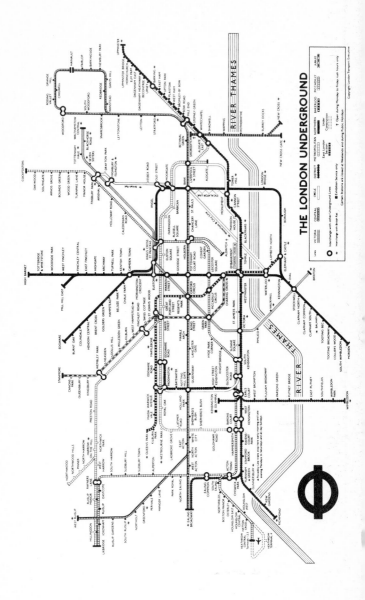

THE LONDON UNDERGROUND